TIME MANAGEMENT

How To Get More Done in a
Multitasking World

Contents

introduction..4

Chapter 1 - Time Management Techniques...............6

Chapter 2 - 15 Efficient Time Management Tips ... 12

Chapter 3 - Time Management For Entrepreneurs26

Chapter 4 - Time Management For Managers........ 36

Chapter 5 - Time Management For Employees...... 43

Chapter 6 - Time Management For Students.......... 49

Chapter 7 - Time Management Tools......................... 58

Chapter 8 - Time Management Do's And Don'ts .. 63

Chapter 9 - Time Management Games...................... 70

Chapter 10 - The Art Of Prioritizing.......................... 75

Chapter 11 - Developing Time Management Skills
.... 79

Chapter 12 - Set Your Goals The Right Way 84

Chapter 13 - Productivity... 87

Chapter 14 - Procrastination.. 92

Chapter 15 - How To Get More Work Done In 2
Hours 96

Chapter 16 - Time Management Faq's 101

Conclusion.. 110

Introduction

I want to thank you and congratulate you for downloading the book, *Time Management: How To Get More Done in A Multitasking World.*

This book contains proven steps and strategies on how to effectively manage your time and accomplish more even if most of your resources are limited.

This compendium consists of sixteen chapters. Time management is clearly defined in the first chapters: the working principles, the basic techniques, and why it is important. Prioritization is likewise defined, and the basic tips on how to do it effectively are enumerated and explained. Also, the reasons why people procrastinate are explained so that readers will know how to avoid it. Productivity levels can also be improved by following simple steps.

You will learn throughout the chapters that no matter what kind of profession or walk of life you belong to, time management is a very important concept. Students, entrepreneurs, managers, and employees – they have varied needs as far as time management is concerned. These are all discussed thoroughly in this book. While passing time, games that will help you develop your skills on time management are also suggested.

Thanks again for downloading this book; I hope you enjoy it!

Chapter 1 - Time Management Techniques

Ask anyone who is successful in his particular field what technique is essential in replicating his feat. Most likely, the answer would be the mastery of time management techniques. Experts say that it is the number one skill that has to be learned, developed, and perfected if one wishes to become really successful in life.

A product of coincidence: that's the fate you will face if you do not have any skills in time management. Your life won't assume a definite direction and you won't be able to lead the direction you wish to take if you are not equipped with the necessary techniques in managing time.

Take control of your life and manage your time with your own hands. With practice coupled with discipline, eventually, you will find that you always have enough time for every task that you need to fulfill.

Mastering techniques in time management is very helpful. Once you get familiar with them, you can achieve more, learn in a faster manner, and be able to play more.

You have more hours of productivity

With better management of time, you have more hours of productivity. This way, you have the tendency to be more disciplined while doing your work. With better time management skills, you veer away from counterproductive things like gossiping, gaming, and idle moments. You have a better sense of direction, and for you, every single second counts.

Think about this: what if you manage to add an extra hour of productivity to your daily timetable. That's an extra five hours per week. Summing up the hours per year, you get to obtain 250 more hours for the whole year. Yes, that's around 6 weeks of work for each year.

What can you do in six weeks? So many things can be achieved successfully if you get to add an extra hour in each workday.

Time is equivalent to money. The more productive time you have, the more earning opportunities you can reap. The possibilities are endless once you master your techniques in time management.

You become more efficient and productive

Aside from getting more hours of productivity, with better time management, you get to learn how to achieve more with less time.

Each one of us is given 24 hours a day. Imagine what you can do, what you can learn, and what you can achieve if you were more efficient and if you were more productive. With the same amount of time, if you turn in more results, you climb up the corporate ladder at a much faster rate.

With better time management, you work at a faster rate without compromising quality. You get to focus more, and you learn how to channel your attention to work. You will be surprised at how rapidly you can progress with less time.

Learn to take control of your life again

With better time management skills and techniques, you can get your life back. You have the upper hand on where your life will be going. Your perception of the future becomes clearer and more exciting because it is crafted by none other than you!

Deadlines will finally stop getting in the way of your socialization. Also, your organization will help you improve your family life because you get to spend more quality time with them. You are spared from the stress that may be brought about by beating a deadline. Instead, you finish ahead of time and reward yourself with some time for relaxation.

Again, flexibility becomes an option and your time becomes a source of comfort, and not stress. You officially take control of your time and someone else no longer controls the way you use it.

Be capable of allocating time for leisure and entertainment

Once you master the art and science of time management, you will be surprised that not only do you have enough time to accomplish all your tasks; you also have extra time to enjoy life, relax, and do some leisure and entertainment activities.

Time management allows you to spend your time the way you wish to spend it. It gives you the privilege to live your life the way you want to. You get to take care of your family more and you also achieve more self-imposed goals.

With that, you will know the true value of relaxation. The result will not only benefit your personal life. A relaxed mind and a relaxed body are more capable of doing more work efficiently.

Now, why do you need to master the techniques of time management? The answer is simple. If you wish to move up the corporate ladder without sacrificing your social, family, and personal life, you need to learn these techniques. Pursue your dreams without sacrificing the things that you consider important.

Chapter 2 - 15 Efficient Time Management Tips

The list of efficient time management tips can go up to hundreds (thousands even). But in this chapter, the top fifteen realistic tips for effective time management are collected, sorted, and discussed to suit your needs.

Everyone encounters time management issues. There are too many tasks, and there is too little time. You can't help but feel stressed the majority of the time. It's as if you have no control of your life; you cannot even think of the things that you consider important. Your work grows more and more demanding and you seem to have no time left for yourself.

But fret no more. In this chapter, you will learn how to sort it out and gain more time for yourself and the things that you consider to be the most important.

You might be thinking at this point: Am I really going to benefit from these time management tips? Okay, it's truly your call, but you might want to give this list of fifteen tips a try. If you spend too much time deciding whether or not you will read through, then that's part of the problem. At this point, you are being challenged to be more decisive to take control of your time and your life again. Remember, time will not slow down so that you can catch up. It is you who should pick up with the pace set by time. If you want things to improve, then you need to do something concrete.

Before being able to do something with time allocation practices, you need to identify what matters to you first and foremost. Those things will be your basis for evaluating your current situation and in planning for the achievement of your goals and values. Once you identify which of your daily activities are truly important to you, you will have an idea of how to approach all your other tasks. Remember, the tips that will be discussed here are just fifteen and most of the lessons that you need to learn will be coming from your own reflections and realizations.

In setting your priorities, you have many considerations. For example, you need to think of your personal values. Use the umbrella analogy. If you have an umbrella and it is raining quite hard, what things in your life would you put under it? The things that you think of at this point are the things that you value. These values shape your goals and the next steps that you will take will depend greatly on them. Activities that need to be prioritized depend greatly on your values and your goals.

If you have a well-defined set of goals, you will find out that your life becomes a bit more harmonious and unified. You will know exactly which plans to pursue and which ones you need to scrap. You will finally realize that you only have twenty-four hours a day and you can't spend them all awake. Therefore, you must only do what's essential so that you can do things in the most efficient and effective manner possible.

At this point, perhaps you already have a clear set of goals in mind. You also have a clear definition of what's essential and what's not. With that, you can apply the fifteen featured time management tips in this chapter.

Efficient time management tip #1: The Priority List

To avoid being a victim of getting sidetracked and being distracted, you need to prioritize. Every time you wake up, remind yourself that you only have a limited amount of time for the day. Have a clear pie chart in mind to help you decide how to divide your time. Decide, as early as possible, how you will allocate your 24 hours. Rank the list of activities in your mind according to how important they are. Put the ones that are urgent and indispensible on top. Position the relatively less important tasks and those that can wait at the bottom of your priority list. Do this every single day and check before you sleep which goals you have accomplished. This will help you prepare properly for the next day.

Efficient time management tip #2: Calendar synchronicity

You have a calendar in your pocket, in your mobile phone, in your laptop, in your desktop, and in a tablet. In order to avoid confusion, make sure to exert some effort in synchronizing your calendar. As much as possible, all the calendars that you have should be of the same version. If synchronization is too difficult for you, keep only two calendars – the first one being the main calendar, and the second one being the back up.

Efficient time management tip #3: Plan to succeed

Make a plan of action for every project or task that you will do. It does not really matter if the project or task at hand is big or small. What you need to make sure is that you are doing things in the most efficient way possible. Have a definite sequence for your project. This sequence will help you point out your progress in every activity that you do. As much as possible, before you begin your project or your tasks, write down this specific sequence. This is analogous to making an outline before writing an essay.

Efficient time management tip #4: Lay your hands on the most important tasks first

According to experts, approaching the tasks that are of utmost importance is the most logical thing to do. Eventually, you will find out that it is really easy to find more time for the ones that are of less importance. Getting distracted by less important tasks will lead to a painful lag in your progress.

Efficient time management tip #5: Keep goals as realistic as possible

A goal needs to be achievable first before you adopt it and put it in your list. Your control over your time will be much better this way. Also, you will have a better chance of reaching your goal. The degree of mastery of a skill is also greater if you put it that way. Being too ambitious won't help you achieve anything. In fact, at best, all it can do is inflate your hollow ego. Instead of burning time trying to grow wings, build a plane instead.

Efficient time management tip #6: Veering away from interruptions

Every workday, you need to block off several hours wherein you choose not to be distracted at all. According to experts, this blocked-off portions should be ideally positioned early in the day. During this period, you need to turn off your gadgets, your mobile phones, your instant and private messengers, your social media notifications, as well as other things that might grab away your focus. This way, you will be able to focus on one task and you have a higher chance of achieving more.

Efficient time management tip #7: Schedule well

Claim the power to schedule your tasks properly and accordingly. Remember that you have in your hands the capability to schedule. As much as possible, put the most important and the most urgent tasks earlier during the day when you still find it easier to focus and you are still alert and energetic. The mundane and the mindless tasks that can wait should be scheduled later in the day. Make sure that you have already finished doing the more important tasks before jumping to less difficult and less urgent ones.

Efficient time management tip #8: Prioritize the unpleasant yet urgent tasks

Unpleasant tasks remain unpleasant no matter how long you delay them. So why prolong the agony? Finish the unpleasant tasks first and be free from the unwanted task in the soonest possible time. Less unpleasant tasks at hand can be equated to greater concentration and focus on other tasks that need to be accomplished.

Efficient time management tip #9: Expect the unexpected

The unexpected always happens, so be prepared for it. That's how life works and if you are more open to the possibility that things won't go as planned, and then you will be spending less time feeling frustrated. With less frustration, the rate of productivity will dramatically increase through the rest of the day. If you think a certain task can be accomplished in 30 minutes, allocate 45. This will help you adjust accordingly. Also, if there is still time to spare after the designated task is accomplished, you can either rest or start the next pending task.

Efficient time management tip #10: Befriend

transition periods

Some people hate waiting time because they believe that it hinders them from being productive. However, given the current state of technology, there is no longer an excuse for staying idle. Even if you are on your way from the office to your home, you can spend the time in the taxi reading through the emails you received and replying to those that you can. Or if you are stuck in traffic, you can do more with your handheld device – schedule dinner meetings or update your task list for the next day. It is your choice – anything that you can accomplish, no matter how big or small that task is, will help you achieve your goals.

Efficient time management tip #11: The 80-20 rule

According to recent research, twenty percent of your efforts are responsible for eighty percent of your outputs. To put it more simply, you need to understand that if you have ten tasks, 8 of those will be a result of 1/5 of your effort. The remaining 4/5 of your effort is usually the distracted kind and it results in the accomplishment of the remaining two tasks. Therefore, if you are going to accomplish something, you need to do the more important ones first before you go to the "distracted phase."

Efficient time management tip #12: Make an effort to take regular breaks

Here's what most productive people do: they do their tasks undistracted for 45 solid minutes. For the rest of the hour, they spend time relaxing, playing around, or pausing. According to studies, a person can only perform at an optimal level for 45 minutes. After that, his performance is bound to go down. So instead of doing work in a non-ideal state, why not take a short break every 45 minutes? Replenish your energy by eating or drinking something, looking at the scenery, or closing your eyes. When you feel that you are ready once again, feel free to go back to your task.

Efficient time management tip #13: Learn to say no

"No" is not a sign of passivity. "No," when used properly is a very powerful word. It can save you time and it can help you focus on the things that matter more to you. While "keeping your hands full" is one common indicator that you are productive, you should not think that taking all the tasks that you can take is a healthy practice. From time to time, you need to say "no" so that the task can be properly and evenly delegated and so that you can be fair to yourself.

Efficient time management tip #14: Forgive yourself for the imperfections

To be truthful, many overachieving individuals find it difficult to accept that perfection is far from being achieved. Trying to be perfect will make all your other tasks be in vain. It is trying to chase the impossibly fast or trying to reach the unbelievably high. Earlier, it was said that you need to set realistic goals. Forgiving oneself for the imperfections is just a continuation of that tip. Know the standards, try to do something that is above what's good enough and embrace the imperfections of your work. That's the healthy way of doing that.

Efficient time management tip #15: Flexibility is the key

Whatever you do and whatever you plan to do are bound to change. Be flexible enough to adjust accordingly. From time to time, on a personal level try out different methods so that you can adopt what works best for you. View schedules as suggestions that may be changed for the better. Do not feel bad if your schedule is not detailed down to the minute. Instead, focus on the tasks that need to be accomplished instead.

With these 15 efficient time management tips, you must have already realized the value of time. Many have said this already and no one can deny that time is money. But more than that, time is life. So do not waste a single second of it.

After all, you cannot create time. What you can do is manage it properly so that you can achieve more within a limited time frame.

Chapter 3 - Time Management for Entrepreneurs

If you are an entrepreneur, you should be familiar with the 2-hour rule. Do you know that for any working day, the first two hours are found to be the most productive hours? Therefore, if you are an entrepreneur, you should line up the most important and the most urgent tasks within your first two hours in the office. During this period, make sure to veer away from the distractions. Avoid looking into your mobile phone or handheld gadget. Upon arriving at your office, avoid logging in to your favorite social media accounts. Also, you should not check your emails or answer incoming calls. This way, you can make the most of your time.

With this strategy, you can juggle the tasks in a better and more efficient manner. As an entrepreneur, you should know how to balance your time so that you can accomplish the large chunks of tasks without overlooking the tasks that are under the "menial" category.

With this, time management for entrepreneurs is an important skill that has to be mastered. This will help you determine if all parts of your business are up and running efficiently. In this chapter, you will learn the common practices of the most successful entrepreneurs.

Time management for entrepreneurs technique #1: Keeping a list

As an entrepreneur, time management is crucial. No task – whether it is big or small – should be overlooked or missed. Therefore, it is crucial to keep a list if you want to successfully juggle the tasks that need to be done. Keeping a priority list does not only help remind a person what to accomplish within a limited period of time, it also assists you in reflecting on the level of priority that each task on the list has.

Time management for entrepreneurs

technique #2: Keeping a journal

If the list gives you a roadmap, the journal will help you keep track of the specific procedures that you have followed. Though others might say that journal keeping will lead you nowhere, experts beg to differ. By keeping a journal, you can take note of your best practices. Also, you get reminded of your tasks if you get the hang of making a daily entry in your journal. It gives you a chance to foresee how you want to do the next tasks that you lined up.

Journal keeping also helps an entrepreneur to break down large chunks of daily tasks into pieces that are bite-size and easier to manage. This way, a definite plan of action can be created ahead of time so that most of the tasks that need to be completed will be accomplished.

Keeping a journal also makes you realize when to take a rest. In the world of business, especially if you have multiple businesses, it is difficult to find a convincing signal that will tell you to relax a bit and take a rest. If you have a journal, according to entrepreneurs who keep one, the point of realization that there is a need to rest comes into mind. This usually occurs when they have already completed a lot of accomplishments for the day.

Time management for entrepreneurs technique #3: Maximizing the potential of technology

Mobile and Internet technology has made the world a lot smaller than how it was a few years back. Thanks to this, entrepreneurs can be in multiple places at the same time, achieving more than what was considered imaginable a decade ago. This way, they can catch the pace of the continuously changing times and be on top of every single task that needs to be accomplished no matter where they are.

Now, even when an entrepreneur is out of town or out of the country for business meetings or is at home taking a break, he can constantly check the progress of the work that needs to be accomplished. There are also mobile applications launched to help in managing businesses.

Also, with the help of technology, entrepreneurs are able to achieve the work and life balance. They get to check on their families more no matter how busy they get. Juggling family and business is a challenging thing especially for entrepreneurs who are managing several businesses. But now, they can talk with their loved ones anytime and anywhere without getting in the way of the businesses – thanks to technology.

Sending real time messages is also possible now. If entrepreneurs find it difficult to express themselves in an email response, they can quickly turn to Skype to clarify things in their businesses. Also, sending IMs instead of making an overseas call has become a very convenient and cost-effective option for entrepreneurs. Such a wonderful thing that comes in for free was not even imaginable twenty years ago.

Time management for entrepreneurs technique #4: Save time in meetings

Any businessman and entrepreneur would agree: the most time-consuming task is attending meetings. Yes, attendance in meetings is quite essential especially if you want to streamline processes in your business or if you want to expand your business; however, scheduling too many meetings or overstaying can be a time-waster.

One tip from the experts: schedule some breathing time in between meetings. Devote these periods to the digestion of the concepts tackled and in making a mind map of what needs to be achieved. It is highly recommended that you allow yourself to understand what was tackled before you move on to the next meeting. In addition, you need to devote at least 50 percent of the actual meeting time for asking questions, clarifying points, and explanation of the concepts in order to maximize understanding. This way, you can be assured that you will reach the highest level of productivity.

Making sure that everyone is on the same page is a regular task that needs to be done by any entrepreneur when attending a meeting. Otherwise, the time devoted to the meeting might be wasted time.

Time management for entrepreneurs technique #5: Learn the value of outsourcing

When done in a correct and efficient manner, you will be surprised with how much time and how much money you are going to save by outsourcing. According to one expert entrepreneur, this is true for both old and new businesses. If your business is relatively new, outsourcing is a wise choice because you will save a lot of time with outsourcing instead of building in-house resources that do not exist yet. However, when you do outsourcing, you need to be very careful in choosing the services to which you subscribe.

Outsourcing is considered to be very valuable for project-based and specialist tasks and duties. This is a good choice especially when the expertise needed is not within your core competencies. Some of the most outsourced services are the following: auditing and accounting, public relations, web design, website development, and graphic arts design.

However, for those that are within the core competencies of your business, make sure to keep them in-house to avoid demoralizing your men and to further hone their talents and competencies. Of course, choose staff who are reliable and skillful enough to pull off what's required of them.

Time management for entrepreneurs technique #6: Learn the value of constant communication and proper delegation

Remember that you are not Superman. Therefore, it is essential to build a reliable and competent team who can pull off the tasks that need to be done on a regular basis. This way, you can manage your time better and you will not think that everything is all on your shoulders.

Ideally, serving the clients, managing the accounts, and selling the products are some of the tasks that you should not do yourself. These are the things that your people can do for you efficiently and correctly. By properly delegating these tasks to the people who can, you will have all the time that you need to review the state of your business's finances, improve or streamline the technique and strategies you are currently utilizing, and develop profitable markets and customers.

But before you delegate, you need to have a

standard in place so that your people will have an idea of what their performances are measured against. In order to do this, you might want to come up with a rubric or expectations and communicate them properly to your staff as well as your clients. Of course, the approach for the staff would be different from the approach for the clients.

Chapter 4 - Time Management for Managers

A successful manager has the innate capability to manage his time well. However, there is a prevailing belief among managers that their managerial skills are already at par. This is wrong. Assuming that your managerial and time management skills are good enough already is not a very healthy outlook. Here's a solution: be task oriented and prepare a plan of action to make the work setup simple and for you to keep track of your effectiveness as a manager for a definite period of time.

Typically, an effective manager plans his day way before it starts in order to maximize his use of time. This will allow him to identify immediately what needs to be accomplished. He will also be able to properly align short-term goals with long-term goals. Therefore, planning ahead is a habit that any aspiring manager should hone, adopt, and master.

However, an effective manager is open-minded enough to recognize the fact that there are factors that are bound to change the factors and elements in your plan, which leads to adjustments. A good manager is able to save time by learning to move on fast. He accepts the fact that a time schedule is borderless and the world, in reality, cannot be defined by the schedule you have set. A good manager is able to come up with a definite plan and schedule. On the other hand, an excellent manager is prepared ten moves ahead. He has alternate plans if the unexpected happens. This way, if ever there should be changes, then he can make an adjustment that won't derail the long-term plan.

Recognize the fact that Murphy's Law does exist. If anything can go wrong, it will at the worst time possible. You need to embrace this fact, and integrate "brush fire" into your daily schedule. However, this should not be tagged "brush fire" per se. You need to integrate it into each task to give some leeway if ever something unexpected happens.

In this chapter, you will learn more about the specific methods of time management that each manager may find useful.

Time Saving Tip for Managers #1: Give an honest evaluation of the weaknesses and strengths of your team

This may be a considerably difficult task because you might hurt some feelings in the process, but this is essential if you want to know exactly how your team is faring in terms of skills. This process is sometimes called the identification of the baseline; the manager needs to be courageous and at the same time eloquent enough to point out the team's strengths and weaknesses. The manager has an option to go down to the individual level. By knowing what your arsenal contains, you will have an idea of what you can expect in-house. By being aware of what's missing, you will know what to outsource. Overall, this is a starting point for any team who aspires to achieve more.

Time Saving Tip for Managers #2: Devote a block of time for meetings

Things are better done if you are not distracted and if they are done continuously. If possible, avoid scheduling meetings at random. It would be a lot better if they were scheduled in blocks. If you can devote an entire day for meetings (with digestion time in between, of course) and leave the rest of the week for other things that matter to you and your business, that would be great! Also, if you schedule meetings within one day, the chance of extending a meeting would be less. Therefore, you will be able to start and end on time. If all the meetings for the week are done in one day, you will find out that it is much easier to layout the next tasks that need to be done.

Time Saving Tip for Managers #3: Pre-

schedule return calls even before the call is received

This simple time saving tip enables the manager to accomplish two things. First, phone calls will not interrupt you and what you are doing. Phone calls can be pretty distracting, so reserve phone calls until later in the day when most of your tasks are already done. Also, you get to adhere to your planned schedule. Next, the secretary who is taking the phone calls will have a definite time to give if callers ask when to expect a phone call back. At least, by pre-scheduling return calls, you will be able to respond to everyone accordingly.

Time Saving Tip for Managers #4: Be crystal clear when it comes to communicating expectations

Managers are not expected to do everything by themselves; therefore, it is essential to delegate tasks to your team. You might be asking why clarity is an emphasized modifier here and what it has to do with your time management effectiveness. Truth be told, many tasks are left undone or half-done simply because the tasks are ambiguous and unclear. Much time is lost to revisions and overhauling, which might have been avoided if the task was clearly communicated to your team. Aside from the specifications of the task, you need to be crystal clear with your expectations. Invite questions and clarifications from your staff if anything is unclear with your instructions and expectations. That way, you will expect nothing but the best from them.

Time Saving Tip for Managers #5: Do some QT

In case you are wondering, QT stands for "quiet time." The best managers schedule a QT every single day and they religiously enforce this as scheduled. They find this as an opportunity to reflect and contemplate on how well they have done their tasks and duties for the day. This is also a time to reflect on what went wrong and what can be done to avoid committing the same mistake. Lastly, they get to plan for the day ahead. During QT, they keep track of their progress, and the managers make a mental picture of how much work has been done and how much more is left to be done.

Chapter 5 - Time Management for Employees

If you are an employee, on the other hand, you also need to employ some strategies to make the most out of your eight-hour shift. This will improve your chances of climbing up the corporate ladder because you get most of your tasks done within a reasonable amount of time without sacrificing the quality of the work that you turn in.

Workers need to learn how to manage their tasks and prioritize certain aspects of work. In the workplace nowadays, workers are required to produce more results than ever. The demand of the workplace has exponentially increased because everything is aided by technology and this can be very exhausting. With limited time every single day, you are expected to do more despite the occasional shortage in resources.

This is where proper time management comes

in. If you don't find the time to develop your time management skills, then you will possibly have a difficult time delivering outputs on time. Worse, you might find yourself missing one meeting after another and all the work piling up on your desk without you knowing. If such a scenario continues for you, sad to say, the company might end up looking for somebody who is more efficient and more reliable than you.

To avoid this, we have listed some time hacks for employees in this chapter.

Employee Time Hack #1: List the small and easy tasks

For starters, you need to look into tasks that you find easy to complete. List them and make sure that you haven't missed anything. This way, you can set them aside for a while and focus on the big tasks first. Since the small tasks you listed can be accomplished quickly compared to others, you can do them later or during a time when you face distractions. Also, this ensures you that you get to accomplish multiple tasks during the course of the day.

Employee Time Hack #2: Break the big task down into small, more manageable ones

This tip will help you identify where to start. Usually, you find it extra challenging to face a big project just because it is too big. To approach this problem, you need to lay your full attention into that project and try to find a way to break it down into bite size chunks. By thinking of a project as an aggregate of many simple tasks, it looks easier to confront, work on, and complete. Remember, no task is too big for an employee who is smart enough to recognize that it can be broken down into smaller and easier tasks.

Employee Time Hack #3: Create your to-do list for the next day before you leave the office

While others are more familiar with the practice of starting the day with making a to-do list, studies have shown that it is not a positive way to begin one's day. It only reminds you of the frustrations for not completing some of your tasks yesterday. But if you do it right before you go home, you can look at the task of making a to-do list in a more hopeful and a more positive perspective. Making this your concluding activity of the day every single day will help you visualize and achieve what you wish to accomplish both in the short-term and the long-term sense.

Employee Time Hack #4: To monitor your personal and professional progress, use a calendar

There are instances wherein you have to schedule way ahead of the designated date. This can be easily overlooked if you are not keeping a calendar. Therefore, if you care enough about keeping track of every single thing that happens in your life, you have to mark it down on your calendar. This way, you become more efficient and your superiors will perceive you as somebody who is very reliable because you do not miss anything that you need to do. Here's another trick that you can do: when using an e-calendar on your mobile device, set an alarm a day before and 15 minutes before so that you are properly reminded of that particular engagement. If you need to do some sort of preparation, given that you were reminded at least a day before, you will have sufficient time to do so.

Employee Time Hack #5: As much as possible, ignore all sorts of distractions

Almost anything can get you off track, so as much as possible retain your focus. Stay away from possible sources of distractions. Ignore your phone and your other mobile devices. Defer checking your Facebook account until later in the day. From time to time, try to take a glance at your to-do list to constantly remind you how much you have already achieved so far. If you are the type who can't resist the urge to give in to distractions, schedule dealing with such for around 15 to 30 minutes of each day. Deal with your distractions and do nothing else. Preferably, schedule this after your lunch break so that you can go full swing with tasks that truly matter afterwards. Just remember, juggling serious work and distractions at the same time can be a bit unhealthy for you and your professional advancement.

Employee Time Hack #6: Avoid multitasking by all means

Many employees think that they are a bit more efficient when they are doing many things at the same time. However, they are wrong. When you do not give your 100 percent to a certain task, chances are you will finish it half-baked. According to experts, multitasking can hurt your level of productivity. Therefore, this proves that human beings are more capable of doing one task effectively at a time.

Chapter 6 - Time Management for Students

It is only you who can tell that you are falling behind in a specific course or learning idea. The instructors and professors generally do evaluation only twice within the semester: one after the midterms and after the last day of your classes. Even the instructors find it impossible to monitor the individual progress of students, so you have to do this for yourself. Thus, it is essential for any student to have the capability to reflect so that the proper action can be taken.

Acceptance is the key. Without accepting that there is a necessity to manage your time properly and efficiently, you cannot do anything about your current situation. But if you choose to do something about it, it might not be too late. The following are the practical ways of catching up in a course:

- Do a thorough self-check. What are

your weaknesses? What are your strengths? Look at your graded academic requirements. What repeatedly rates unsatisfactorily? By doing a thorough self-check, you get to have an idea on how to divide your time outside your class time. Devote solid hours for academic endeavors.

- Attend all classes religiously. As much as possible, avoid missing a single class. An hour and a half's worth of lecture missed might lead to more serious backlogs that are impossible to make up for.

- Schedule absences only when absolutely necessary. Here, you should not limit reasons to being sick or attending to emergency situations. You can use your absences in a more time-efficient sense. You can use your absences to study for a major exam or to finish an assignment or project that requires special attention.

- Consult your instructor or professor regularly. This simple gesture is actually taken as a good sign by your instructor. It usually means that at least, you are trying your best to catch up and learn. You can save time by doing this instead of wondering how to do something that you do not really understand.

- Make a definite daily schedule. If you are currently devoting 2 hours daily study time and it looks like it is not enough, do not hesitate to make it double. Also, make sure that your schedule is flexible enough to accommodate new tasks that are assigned to you in class.

- It might help if you will get a study partner or if you will participate in study groups. This way, you will have someone to ask if you do not understand the lessons.

- Use the University's learning resource center. Use it as often as you wish. Use it as often as necessary. Such facilities should not be taken for granted in any manner. They are meant for students who are having a hard time coping with their lessons.

- Eliminate distractions. Reserve the time for television after you study. Ignore the other gadgets you have if you are still doing your assignment. As much as possible, give your studies undivided attention in order to get the best results.

- If possible, visit the nearest bookstore to get additional resources. There are study guides available there. In some instances, there are recommended textbooks that are easier to follow than the one recommended by your instructor.

- You should befriend people who excelled in the subject area that you are currently having a hard time in. Being nice to these people has a lot of benefits, you know.

- Get a tutor. It can be a friend who is willing to do it for free or a pro tutor who does it for a living. Either way, you should maximize the opportunity. Ask all the questions that you think you need to ask. Ask for sufficient examples and illustrations. You might also want to ask for take home assignments to check if you truly understand.

- Devote time for breaks. Not taking a break can be unhealthy and it is absolutely normal for students like you to party every now and then. But remember not to overdo it because it can be counterproductive.

These are just some of the suggestions. Hopefully, these will help you get back on track again. Dealing with academics is not an easy thing. Therefore, you should be putting more of your attention to it.

Do not fret if you are still unsure of the career path that you intend to take after you graduate from the University. You are not alone. Many University students are pursuing their different courses only to be struck by a realization that they want to do something else with their lives.

Also, you need to make sure that you are not wasting the next four years of your life doing something that you do not intend to practice in the long run. The best time management technique that any student can learn is the skill of planning his career ahead of time. Time wasted studying something you do not like is equivalent to an entire life wasted.

Career planning might help a lot and this should be done as early as possible. Most high schools are actually sponsoring these kinds of activities to help incoming college freshmen to plan their careers as early as possible. After all, after graduation, you are bound to spend the largest chunk of your life making a living. Therefore, as much as possible, do something to make your next 40 years a delightful ride.

The following are some of the tried and tested career planning tips and tricks that work:

- Go directly to the office for Career Counseling in your University. Set an appointment with them and express your intention. There are people in that office who are experts in career planning and they will know exactly what advice to give you.

- Take assessment exams that can point out your career goals and interests. The questions can be fun to answer: "Do you like playing chess or playing contact sports like basketball?" These examinations will help you know yourself better.

55

- They can also simulate the Human Resources Department environment so that you will get the feel of what it is like to be interviewed. They will share with you the tips and tricks in order to go through the application process with ease and confidence.

- From the same office, they will teach you how to prepare the most impressive resume. Also, you can learn about how to make a cover letter.

- The same office has vast knowledge about available internships connected to your degree program. From an internship, you will get a general feel of what it is like to work along the lines of your degree program. After the internship, you can say whether you liked the experience or not.

- They can help you build your letters of reference from people in authority. These are especially helpful because these people will help you in proving that you have what it takes to qualify for the job that you are applying for.

- If you are afraid to face an interviewer, you can practice in the University's Career Counseling Office. They are willing to do simulation interviews for you. This will save you time because you will get to minimize the number of failed interview efforts in the future.

- The University also holds a regular job fair. They can help you in networking your way to a good job without having to spend excess money, effort, and time. And the most amazing part is that they are doing it for free.

Maximize the opportunity and follow these career planning tips and tricks. These can help you in landing the best job and at the same time, this will help you manage your time well while you are in the university.

Chapter 7 - Time Management Tools

Time management is truly essential in achieving success. This includes having a planner and listing tasks that you need to accomplish within a limited period of time. In this chapter, you will learn more about the necessary tools that you can use to make the most of your time.

Each of the tools discussed in this chapter are easy to learn, use, adopt, and master. In the long run, you will personally know how much time you are able to save just by using these.

Time Management Tool #1: The Master List and the Time Planner

The time planner is often overlooked by ordinary people thinking that they can take note of their plans in their heads. But remember not to trust your rusty memory especially if you are bound to accomplish a lot of tasks. Your life should be kept as organized as possible. Without a time planner, you will find everything in the wrong place and you don't get to achieve much.

Did you know that the best binder enables you to plan your entire year, each month of the year, each week of the month, each day of the week, and each hour of the day? That's one quality that you have to look for in your time planner.

Having a good planner is one thing, and making specific entries in that time planner is another. As much as possible, you need to write down entries that are clear and complete. This holds true if you are putting down a task that needs to be done a few weeks or a few months from now. As much as possible, the entry should encapsulate the main goal and the expected action from you so that when you read it a few months from now, you will know exactly what needs to be done.

Time Management Tool #2: The Daily To-Do List

You have seen this recur in the earlier chapters, but you might be wondering how working from a list really works. It is like doing a daily list of tasks while maximizing your optimal productivity rate. From these bits of information, you get to learn what you want to do in the long run and what you are capable of doing within a specified time frame.

Did you know that according to studies, making a daily to-do list helps you increase your output by a whopping twenty-five percent? If that's the case, you tend to be more relaxed and you are able to eliminate the much-unwanted stress. By having a to-do list, you get to be more productive, become more fulfilled, and become less frustrated. You tend to be more motivated to accomplish more given this kind of mindset.

Time Management Tool #3: The Time

Management System

If you have a smart phone or any handheld gadget, you can easily download any time management system that suits your need and your taste. Commonly tagged as PDAs or the personal digital assistants, these applications are digital systems that help you plan your time effectively, which lets you achieve more efficiently. It does not matter what field you are actually into, these PDAs do wonders. You can even install these PDAs in a synchronized manner in your laptop, smartphone, and other handheld devices.

Time Management Tool #4: The Forty-five File System

This is a wonderful thing that is practiced by the most driven and accomplished people of today. This method gives you the capability of organizing your life for the next two years. Twenty-four months can be too large of a timeframe, you might think, but it bears a lot of advantages. For example, it will encourage you to make long-term goals. It can push you to enroll in a Master's degree program or other short courses. With the forty-five file system, you envision what you want to happen in your life for the years ahead.

You might be wondering what exactly is contained in the forty-five file system. The first thirty-one files correspond to the 31 days of the current month. Meanwhile, the next 12 files correspond to each month of the year, from January to December. The last two files are devoted for the two years that follow. Adding 31, 12, and 2 gives you 45.

Chapter 8 - Time Management Do's and Don'ts

In this chapter, you will learn more about the favorite do's and don'ts that the most effective individuals abide by. The contents of this compilation are actually adopted by managers, entrepreneurs, employees, and students.

This list has been applauded by many for being very practical, insightful, and achievable. This will save you hours and hours of your day. Many have already expressed their gratitude for knowing the contents of this simple list, so take the time to read, reflect, practice, and master what it communicates.

If you are currently overwhelmed by the many tasks that fill your limited time, this might be the solution that you have been looking for. Now, let us look into the list.

Do think that there's enough time

Always remind yourself that you have enough

time. This will motivate you to achieve a lot within a limited period of time. Dwelling on the possibility that there might not be enough time to finish the task at hand will only give you more excuses not to continue with the task, hence restraining yourself from prioritizing and taking concrete action. This syndrome is called paralysis by analysis, which is very unhealthy when it comes to your productivity.

Always do think that there is sufficient time. When facing a nearing deadline, learn to be calm, connected, and clear. With that, you will know that you can still be productive and efficient and you will realize that the depletion of time is actually something that you can take advantage of. With limited time resources, you can shine. Beating the deadline despite the limited nature of time gives you more reason to feel accomplished and to celebrate your success.

Do try switching your gears

Switching gears in between activities makes you feel that your tasks are not at all monotonous. This way, you do not get tired of what you are currently doing. This will allow you to freshen up and become more productive after doing a certain task or duty.

Do not think, however, that switching gears will not take up time. Therefore, when you make your schedule, the transition period should also be properly allocated for. This will make your plans more realistic.

Do spend time on preparation

In order to be more effective in whatever it is that you are currently doing, make sure that you devote a certain portion of your time for making concrete plans and strategizing the next actions that you are going to take. Don't worry because if this is done properly and without any distractions, you will only have to spend a little less than ten minutes each day to do this.

Don't say yes to everything. Whenever you feel uncertain about the possibility of completing a certain task at hand, simply say, "Allow me to get back to that later". This will communicate to the requester that perhaps, you have other priorities at hand. For sure, they will understand and they will make the necessary action in connection to the request.

Do make a schedule of tasks

Making a schedule is a healthy habit. Whenever you receive a new task, look at the due date and move it accordingly to your time management system. This will help you plan out and divide your time accordingly.

However, if you receive new tasks, do not enter them into your schedule right away. Consider turning down tasks that might destroy your pre-scheduled plan. That way, you will find yourself less stressed. Also, you will accomplish more tasks.

Do conduct an assessment of your priorities

As much as possible, constantly assess if you have your priorities right. Each day you face new opportunities and you must place them side by side with your current priorities. Commit only to the tasks that are actually in line with your goals and priorities. Think of your professional and personal sense of return on investment. Are you going to derive something good out of it? Can you truly commit to it given the current tasks that keep you busy? Don't think that you are a super human who can answer to everything. On a regular basis, revisit your priorities and make sure to do the necessary tweaking.

Do adopt a sense of decisiveness

Indecisiveness and the lack of resolution won't lead you anywhere. So instead of getting overwhelmed by the existence of crossroads, why not think of your priorities and act on them accordingly? Decide right away before time runs out. But do consider your skill set, your resources, and your time whenever you make a decision.

In addition, every time you do a task, aspire for excellence and not for perfection. Strive for what's real and not for the ideal. You will save more time and you will achieve more if you stick to these principles.

Do set goals and aspire to capture them all

This starts with your planning process. Whenever you plan, do not merely list tasks. Look at the larger picture and translate these tasks into goals. Proper goal identification will help you spell out the necessary steps that will help you accomplish the tasks that are in line with your short-term and long-term goals.

However, do not be confused between goal setting and scheduling. Scheduling only addresses surface-level issues while goal setting digs into something deeper. But you are correct if you are driven by the mindset that both activities will help you avoid wasting your time.

Now, time to digest the contents of the list. There's a lot of wisdom communicated here. For sure, as a person who values time, you will derive something useful from the list and apply it in your daily life. In the process, you will learn more about how to streamline your current practices so that you will achieve success and overcome any kinds of challenges.

Chapter 9 - Time Management Games

Everyone deserves some game time. But if you want to be more efficient in using your limited time, make sure that the games that you play to pass your time will help you realize time's true worth and importance.

Note that in this chapter, the games that were chosen are not only meant to teach you what time management is; they will also help you unwind, relax, and have fun. In all the games featured here, you will need to complete several tasks (of increasing difficulty as you move up) against the clock. Every single time you meet the objective, you will see your character's level go up, and face a new challenge. Much like in real life – you face a challenge, surpass it, and you move up one level. You become more capable of facing more difficult challenges.

Without much ado, here's the list. For sure,

you will find one that you will find fun and useful, too. However, you must only limit your playing time to a few minutes each day. This is highly recommended as you commute.

Time Management Game #1: Diner Dash

As of today, thousands have rated Diner Dash with 5 star ratings. There is a free version and a deluxe version. Even if you are on the free version, you should not worry at all. You will obtain the same benefit of the paid version. The goal of this game is quite simple: you only need to manage your restaurant and serve your customers before they lose their temper. However, each level has inherent constraints. These are the challenges that you need to conquer. This is definitely a must-try.

Time Management Game #2: Cooking Dash

From the same makers of Diner Dash, this game belongs to the Dash series. If you are playing Diner Dash for quite some time, you will find Cooking Dash not just as a good alternative, but a complementary game. Here, you need to help Flo and her Granny to keep their multiple restaurants up and running. Otherwise, they will not get the profits. Fully integrated with popular social networking websites, you can even update your friends about your progress.

Time Management Game #3: Jane's Hotel

In this time management game, you have the privilege of running a 5-star hotel. Again, the primary constraint here is the limited time. At the beginning of your game, you have a 2-star hotel. Every time you successfully serve a customer, your reputation will go up and your hotel will be more famous. Doesn't that sound familiar? Isn't it the same in real life?

Time Management Game #4: Supermarket Management

If you dream of owning your own supermarket, then this is your chance to do so

– at least within the premises of the game. Again, you need to beat the clock so that you can earn profits, buy upgrades, and hire people who will help you run your supermarket. As you move up, you will be able to purchase additional shops. And yes, that will mean additional income for you.

Time Management Game #5: Ada's Hospital

With Ada's Hospital, you get to learn how it is like managing a medical unit. The chief constraints here are time and money. You have to successfully run the hospital despite dwindling funds and limited time. Here, you have to do some checkups on customers and carry out laboratory tests. You have to do this fast so that you will not piss off your patients.

Time Management Game #6: Wedding Dash

If you are already tired of restaurants and parallel settings, you might want to try Wedding Dash. Here, all you have to do is extend the necessary assistance to couples who are about to get married. You should act like an expert when it comes to cakes, flower, and other wedding needs.

Time Management Game #7: Sally's Spa

The setting is the relaxing Laguna Beach and your primary role here is to manage a virtual spa. You need to help customers relax and take a rest. Help them reduce stress by giving them face masks, offering sauna baths, and giving them a massage. You have to do all of this within a limited time frame.

These are just some of the time management games that you can choose from. The best thing about most of these games is that you can save your progress. Therefore, if you need to go back to what you are currently doing with your work or your studies, you can immediately stop and save the level you are in. By the way, there are many other games with a similar concept. This will give you a perfect venue for practice.

Chapter 10 - The Art of Prioritizing

Prioritization is an art. It takes practice to perfect. It cannot be learned from the books. Usually, we learn it the hard way. But of course, we all benefit from the sharing of the experts, right? In this chapter, you will learn more about what experts have to say about prioritization, why it is important and how it should be done.

Step 1: The list

In any order, list the tasks that you need to accomplish. You can write it on a small tickler or type it on your laptop. As a rule, list everything in any order and put everything that needs to be accomplished – in work, at home, and in your personal life.

Step 2: Cull out

From the list of everything that you want done, cull out those that are only driven by your personal desires. Focus on your needs and eliminate everything that you can associate with your wants. Also, ask yourself: Is this particular item necessary? If it is, but is of less importance, you can always "demote" it and put it at the bottom of your list.

Step 3: Eliminate entries that can be delegated

If other people can do it for you, take the pleasure of handing over the duty to them. It saves you time and it helps you do other more important things. Also, if you can find any other entries that can be delegated, cross them out and delegate accordingly. In the process of delegating tasks, do not forget to empower your people and let them feel that you trust them with the tasks wholeheartedly. Air your expectations clearly, too.

Step 4: Write down the deadlines

It is absolutely necessary to put all the tasks in one column and indicate the deadlines on the other. Arrange them accordingly so that you will know how to approach the situation. Which tasks depend on the tasks that you delegated? What tasks can you do alone? Here, you can assess the importance of tasks on a day-to-day basis with the help of these deadlines.

Step 5: Estimate

Make an approximation of how long it will take for you to complete a task. Make sure to be consistent when it comes to the units that you will use. The most practical would be in hours.

Step 6: Begin doing the tasks at hand

Constantly keep your hands full. Upon identifying the priorities, you need to start working. With the better-defined priorities, you will find it easier to make the most important decisions. You will not only be able to successfully divide your time, you will also learn to budget your energy.

Step 7: Learn to concentrate

Having a sense of focus is very important in increasing your productivity as well as your efficiency. With proper concentration, you can be sure of two things: (1) that you have accomplished the task; and (2) that you did it right.

Step 8: Do something to avoid interruptions

Impeding the flow of your energy might hurt your productivity. Interruptions can be anything – a person, a thing, or a message. Put these things at the bottom of your list.

Step 9: Know when not to promise anything

Most successful individuals never promise anything, but they try their best to deliver. This helps them earn their credibility and reliability. For example, if you were asked to finish something in 5 days, try huddling for 7 days. But deliver the results in 5 days anyway.

With these nine steps, you can finally say that, indeed, you are on top of all the tasks that you need to accomplish.

Chapter 11 - Developing Time Management Skills

Developing time management skills is a lifelong process. You need to hone these skills continuously and with active and conscious efforts. Mastery of these skills is like chasing an ideal, it is near impossible. But that does not mean that you will stop trying.

So what exactly are the time management skills that you need to develop? Here's a simplified list.

Time Management Skill #1: Setting Goals

You need to master the skill of goal setting. Goals need to be SMART – S-pecific, M-easureable, A-chievable, R-ealistic, and T-ime-bound. However, you can't jump into making goals without doing the necessary prerequisites. To be clear, you should carefully assess the situation at hand and assess what needs to be achieved within the set time. Next, in setting goals, give leeway for flexibility. Prepare for contingency measures.

Time Management Skill #2: Identification of the components of a big task

It takes talent to identify the small parts that make up a big task. But you can learn this with practice. By learning how to do so, you can take small but sure steps towards your goal. And the good thing is you can distribute the other pieces to people who are willing to help.

Time Management Skill #3: Knowing when to take a rest and reward oneself

Believe it or not, taking regular breaks and rewarding oneself can improve a person's performance. It also helps one achieve more and become more efficient.

Time Management Skill #4: Honing a never say die spirit

It will definitely not be all laurels for you. Sometimes, you will face failures and frustrations. More often than not, you will have to deal with backlogs. But take heart and learn to adopt a never say die attitude. This way, you learn to rise from your weaknesses and limitations.

Time Management Skill #5: Dealing with pressure

Have grace whenever you are faced with a big task. Never bow down to pressure. See it as a motivation instead of being a source of stress. From time to time, take a break and relax. Remember, pressure won't go away if you succumb to it. Deal with it well and see good things coming your way.

Time Management Skill #6: Observe patterns with your use of time

Identify your peak time and label it as your prime time. Also, take note of those periods when you feel most distracted. Assess the kinds of activities where you waste your time and keep track of which ones are recurring. Of course, do something about it.

Time Management Skill #7: Routine development

Developing a regular routine for your work proves to be truly beneficial. In line with that, you need to keep your workspace as clean and as organized as possible, too. Also, you need to make a standard schedule for each of your workdays. Write down the details in case there are adjustments.

Time Management Skill #8: Time logging

A time log helps you avoid putting your precious minutes and hours to waste. In the process, all you need to do is to create a chart for the entire week (divided into days). The days will be divided into intervals of half an hour. For the next seven days, you should make it a point to note everything that you will do. After seven days, examine the time log closely to look out for periods wherein you could have been more productive. Also, you will see where your consistent "prime time" is and schedule your next tasks according to your findings.

Chapter 12 - Set your Goals the Right Way

In this chapter, you will learn how to set your goals properly. Note that people are able to perform in a better manner and they are able to achieve more with well-defined goals at hand.

However, you need to examine your goals and why you commit to each. The level of a person's commitment actually depends greatly on three things: (1) the outcomes that are expected from the goals; (2) the person's belief that the goal can be achieved, and (3) the goal setter's level of commitment to other people.

Here, you will learn more about the factors that need to be considered in setting any goal.

Goal Setting Factor #1: The Feedback Mechanism

To see if the goals are constantly being achieved, there should be someone assigned to monitor the progress. Aside from monitoring the progress, he should also provide a feedback mechanism to give evaluation. Without a mechanism for feedback, it would be impossible for people to determine whether or not they are doing things right.

Goal Setting Factor #2: The Complexity of the Task

Before you include any task in your set of goals, you need to assess if you can meet its demands. The chance of succeeding decreases as the level of complexity of the task increases.

Goal Setting Factor #3: Considerations in setting goals and the process of setting them

If you involve more people in the process of setting each goal, there is a greater chance that they will "own" the goal and do everything that they can to see it through. As opposed to something that is imposed, goals that are set together are achieved together.

Goal Setting Factor #4: The proximity of success and the difficulty of the goal

This is derived loosely from TMT or the Temporal Motivation Theory. This theory identifies proximity and goal difficulty as precursors of goal setting. This implies that factors like temporal discounting and the principle of diminishing returns are considered greatly in goal setting. Also, one has to remember that the aggregate parts, once assembled, can result in something greater than the whole.

Chapter 13 - Productivity

In order to boost productivity, this chapter presents the top ten tips for achieving more, gaining greater profits, finishing designated tasks way ahead of time, and accomplishing the goals set.

Productivity Top Tip #1: Most important things first then first things first

This rule is the foolproof solution whenever you are faced with the dilemma of delivering results for multiple activities. But then again, you can consult the chapter on Prioritization to learn more tricks on how this can be done properly.

Productivity Top Tip #2: Get up as early as possible

This will not only help you achieve more early in the day, it also assures that you eat your breakfast, do your exercise, and follow your usual routine. Assuring yourself that these are all done will help you freshen up. These will also better prepare you for the challenges that you will face for the rest of the day.

Productivity Top Tip #3: When writing a task list, use simple words

This will help you condition your mind that the tasks at hand are within your reach. Goals written with complicated words and sentences are often intimidating and discouraging. If you want to avoid that, try to translate the essence of the task in the simplest manner possible.

Productivity Top Tip #4: Eliminate all the clutter

The physical influences the psychological, the mental, and the emotional aspects of a person. Therefore, if you are working in a disorganized workplace, you will find everything distracting. To avoid this, you must simplify and clear out the workspace, leaving behind only what's essential.

Productivity Top Tip #5: Try going to work earlier than what's required

Those who have tried going to their offices and workspace 30 minutes or 1 hour before the start of their shifts agree that they are able to finish more tasks compared to those who come on time. This is because of the fact that they are faced with fewer distractions. There are virtually no people around yet and the phones are not yet ringing like crazy. You also get the chance to spend your quality quiet time for yourself.

Productivity Top Tip #6: Nothing is concretely achieved during meetings

Hence, the suggestion: avoid attending meetings. Minimize time allocated for meetings. But if you are compelled to attend, make it as productive and as effective as possible. Ask questions, if you must, and if you are going to air a suggestion, express it as clearly as possible.

Productivity Top Tip #7: Stick to your TOR or Terms of Reference

Whenever possible, review your Terms of Reference at work. Whenever your boss gives you a task that is not within the bounds of your TOR, learn to say no. This will save you time because you can easily get away from all those unnecessary tasks.

Productivity Top Tip #8: Start with the difficult

Adhering to this principle will make you realize that things are getting better and better because tasks are becoming more and more manageable.

Productivity Top Tip #9: Try to stay offline whenever you do your work

Disconnecting your connection to the Internet

might prove to be an excellent decision because it will help minimize or eliminate distractions. With minimal distractions, you might be surprised with your own progress.

Productivity Top Tip #10: Stick to a job that you are passionate about

An old saying tells us: if your work involves doing something that you truly love, then you won't be working for the rest of your life. Your passion counts as a factor, so consider it before signing up for a job.

Chapter 14 - Procrastination

An old Spanish proverb says that "tomorrow" is the most hectic day of the week. This is because of the usual attitude of many people. Thinking that you can deal with your unfinished business tomorrow will result in a more complicated case. When that happens, things become a bit more complicated and it will be more difficult to deal with.

The keyword here is procrastination. This should not be mistaken as taking a rest. Procrastination is the deliberate "effort" to set aside tasks that can be done right here, right now. In this chapter, you will learn some procrastination killers.

Procrastination Killer #1: Move

Some people don't progress because they fail to move. These people tend to be "paralyzed" because they tend to overthink. Instead of burning those precious hours daydreaming, why not start taking action that will help you get nearer to the finish line?

Procrastination Killer #2: No task is difficult enough

If you wish to conquer a specific task effectively, then you need to tell yourself that it is doable. Telling yourself otherwise won't help a bit because it will merely discourage you.

For someone who is talented and persevering enough, no task is impossible to complete.

Procrastination Killer #3: Take the first baby step

It does not really have to be a frog's leap. You do not even have to pole vault. Ideally, what you need to do is to take a small step forward to cause a domino effect. Once you officially commence a particular task, you tend to have the drive to complete it. According to another old saying, a journey begins with a single step.

Procrastination Killer #4: Follow the downhill pattern

Of course, you have to climb the mountain first before you go downhill. This means that you have to begin with the more difficult tasks first. That way, you will not only have the sense of accomplishment – you will also feel like things are getting more and more manageable.

Procrastination Killer #5: When encountering a crossroad, decide which turn to take

By deciding right away on which turn to take, you will have enough time to go back and correct your actions just in case the turn you took is the wrong turn. Being indecisive wastes a great deal of time, so try to make decisions right away.

Procrastination Killer #6: Just face your fears

Facing your fears is saying yes to success.

Giving in to procrastination is like fearing success. Assess your strengths and weaknesses and decide if your fears are reasonable. Sometimes, you will be surprised to find out that your fears are unfounded. Also, identify if it is truly a fear or if it is simply the unwillingness to leave your comfort zone. Either way, take the appropriate action in order to succeed.

Procrastination Killer #7: Finish what you have begun

Taking the first step is one thing; taking the last one is another. If you do not want to have any regrets, do yourself a favor. Finish everything that you have started. Do not quit. Quitting will give you the worst nightmares.

Chapter 15 - How to Get More Work Done in 2 Hours

Statistically, the first two hours at work is considered to be the most productive. It does not matter what profession you are in. As someone who is aspiring to be more productive in his day job, one has to make some active efforts in order to maximize the first two hours of the day.

Starting the day right will definitely help you achieve a lot. Aside from the tips that were already presented in the previous chapters, you need to remember some important principles. The principles included in this list were taken from more experienced and more successful individuals. Their insights are compiled to help you understand how important the first two hours of your workday are.

1. **A clean slate gives you a fresh start.** This is what the first two hours can

provide you. Whatever it is that made you feel like crap yesterday, forget it. Forgive yourself for your shortcomings and your underperformance yesterday. Today is a new day so you always have a chance to make up for your inadequacies.

2. **Stabilize your mood.** Being moody will get you nowhere; it would be better if you will try to get in touch with your emotions and your moods and see how it becomes a factor to the people around you. By being aware of your mood's effect on others, you will be compelled to change for the better. Also, starting your day with the right attitude will help you adopt the proper attitude for the rest of the day.

3. **To achieve more in the first two hours, be present.** This means that you need to be present not just physically, but mentally and emotionally as well.

This is important so that you can communicate your thoughts and your feelings adequately if solicited. Also, this will help you give your 100 percent to completing any task at hand.

4. **In your first two hours, make sure to take advantage of a clear and refreshed mind.** A lot of experts agree that the brain works best early in the morning. Your creative juices tend to overflow during the first two hours of the day, so you should not allow them to go down the drain.

5. **Respond only to the urgent email conversations and to important phone calls.** For the rest that are not "urgent" and important, try to respond in the latter part of the day.

6. **In your first two hours, be constantly reminded of your core purpose.** Having a clear sense of purpose helps you come up with a clear direction.

Being clear with your sense of purpose can help you maintain your level of motivation. That way, you will be more inspired to achieve your goals.

7. **Devote ten to fifteen minutes to organizing your workspace.** As much as possible, keep your desk clear. Think of a better way to organize your things. This will help you in setting the tone for the rest of this day. Having a clear and organized workspace will help you avoid confusion. And of course, that will save you a lot of time.

8. **Have a short chat with your colleagues.** It is important to ask them what they are up to for the day. Within ten to fifteen minutes, you can clearly express your plans. Also, if you need help from any of them, you can easily ask. By keeping track of the goals of the team, you will maintain your level of commitment and motivation. More

importantly, you will establish the necessary connections that are needed in the workplace.

9. **Conclude your first two hours with a well-deserved break.** After working hard for two straight hours, you need to assess your progress. That's why it is essential to take a break because it will help you maintain your level of momentum.

Having a clear 2-hour routine every morning helps you develop healthy habits that you will need in raising your level of productivity. Morning is the best period for honing your time management skills and in setting the mood for the rest of the day. In maximizing the 2-hour timetable, you need to be focused and optimistic.

Chapter 16 - Time Management FAQ's

15 Questions & Answers

We all try to be more productive than what we currently are. However, inasmuch as we want to be hyper-productive, it is just too difficult to even try. But at least, you can improve your productivity quotient little by little. With your best efforts, you know that you can become a better time manager if you will give it a try.

However, despite the thoroughness and the comprehensive nature of the previous chapters, some questions are left unanswered. In this particular chapter, some of the top questions will be answered in the best way possible. This part of the compendium will feature the top fifteen frequently asked questions (FAQ) about time management and improving productivity.

FAQ #1: Which is more beneficial: working hard or working smart? Why?

Working hard is something that is truly admirable; however, if you want to achieve more in life, you have to work smart. This holds true for any kind of career.

In approaching any task, working smart is beneficial because you have more freedom to explore ways on how to accomplish the task without experiencing burnout. When you work hard, chances are, you work like a robot and that can be pretty exhausting. But if you work smart, you save time, effort, money and all other resources.

Note that the rationale of managing one's time is not due to the desire to schedule more tasks within a single day; it is about finding ways to do tasks faster without sacrificing the quality of the output.

FAQ #2: Why is prioritization important?

Prioritization is important because it helps you complete the tasks that are considered to be the most pressing first. When you map out your activities within the day, you need to pinpoint two to three crucial tasks that require your attention the most. After identifying these tasks, you know that you have to address them first.

FAQ #3: Why is "no" considered to be a strong word in time management?

While it is great if you can juggle several tasks at a time, you need to understand that your capabilities and your resources are limited. Therefore, if you do not want to experience stress, you need to choose your tasks carefully. In the process, you will have to learn the art of saying "no" to save yourself from the stress and frustration.

FAQ #4: How is a full night's sleep connected to time management?

Sacrificing sleep just to make up for the backlog is not a healthy practice. It will not only hurt your physical health, it will also hurt your productivity. Giving yourself around seven to eight hours of sleep helps optimize the function of your body and your brain. On the other hand, not having enough sleep will put your efforts to manage your time in vain.

FAQ #5: Is there a particular trick to achieve focus or concentration?

Truth be told, there is none in particular, really. But closing all your windows for browsing can be a start. In addition, putting the phone and other handheld devices inside the bag or the drawer might also help. Turning on the music, if this is particularly helpful to you, is allowed. When you put your mind into the task, make sure to imagine that nothing else in the world exists – just you and the task. Immerse yourself into it until it's done.

FAQ #6: Why should I start early?

The response here is simply: to finish early. Quite pragmatic, isn't it? Think of your favorite ball game. The teams are always eyeing for an early lead so that eventually, they will not be stressed towards the end game. Post-game analysis shows that most teams that are able to establish an early lead win the game. The same is true with us. Those who are into starting early are more likely to succeed in finishing the task.

FAQ #7: What details should matter when carrying out a task?

The rule here is simple: never allow an unimportant and insignificant detail to bug you. Though it is good that you have a keen sense of detail, sometimes, you have to let go of being a perfectionist. It saves you time and it allows you to move on. Know your standards, beat them, but do not waste excessive time perfecting every single detail.

FAQ #8: What is an effective way of forming useful habits?

First, you need to identify your key tasks. These key tasks are the ones you will likely form eventually into a habit. For example, if you are a blogger, then you write. You make sure that you write excellently. If you do this repeatedly and regularly, it becomes a habit. In order to make good things out of this habit, you try to practice on a regular basis, too. With time, make it a point to turn the key task into something that's more than a habit. Make it your leisure activity too, so that it will come in naturally and for sure, you'll enjoy it more than you usually do.

FAQ #9: Self-imposed deadline: How effective are they?

According to experts, the proper mindset for doing any task is "I will finish this task in x hours" instead of "I will work on this task until it is through." Giving yourself a self-imposed time constraint gives you the healthy kind of pressure. It also gives you some extra time once you beat the self-imposed deadline. It pushes you to concentrate on the task and do it in the most efficient manner possible.

FAQ #10: Why is the in-between task buffer important?

The downtime that usually happens in between major tasks should be treated as a reward. Let your brain cells breathe a bit. If time is sufficient, walk around, clear your mind, and meditate. This will refresh your disposition for the next task.

FAQ #11: Is personal health a part of the time management and productivity plan?

Definitely! According to studies, a healthy body is definitely more productive. Therefore, you should do your best to eat healthy, to exercise, and to get sufficient rest.

FAQ #12: What is meant by: "By doing less, you accomplish more"?

This is one way of saying: avoid doing the things that don't really count in the long run. Also, you need to focus and concentrate at the tasks that need to be done. This will also help you avoid wasting time due to confusion. By focusing on less, you get to achieve more. Focus on fewer tasks that bear greater value. Avoid those many tasks that are hollow.

FAQ #13: What is the general rule in spending an effective time manager's weekend?

Of course, you need to devote most of your weekend to rest. That's what weekends mainly are for. But do not hesitate to bring home some work. By working 2-4 hours on a

Saturday and around 1-2 hours on a Sunday, you will be able to address your backlogs or work on something in advance. This will make you excited to face Monday.

FAQ #14: What is the rule on related tasks?

There is no specific rule on related tasks. But as much as possible, accomplish related tasks together. If not together, try to schedule them one after another. The common mindset will help you get through it efficiently and get through it fast.

FAQ #15: Why is commitment necessary?

Commitment is necessary to have a sense of ownership. It will also give you a feeling of accomplishment, professionalism, and resolution. The sense of commitment will take you a long way.

Conclusion

Thank you again for downloading this book!

I hope this book was able to help you with time management issues, irrespective of the walk of life to which you belong.

Now, what needs to be done is to put what you have learned to action.

Finally, if you enjoyed this book, please take the time to share your thoughts and post a review on Amazon. It'd be greatly appreciated!

Thank you and good luck!

33322168R00064

Made in the USA
Lexington, KY
22 June 2014